Pinterest Marketing for Authors
and
FREE Bonus – Video Marketing for Authors

By Diana Loera

Additional Books by Diana Loera

What I Did to Sell More Kindle Books on Amazon

What I Did to Sell More Kindle Books on Amazon Book 2

What I Did to Sell More Kindle Books on Amazon Book 3 Pay to Play

Fast Start Guide to Flea Market Selling

USA Based Wholesale Directory 2015

Insider's Guide to Scrapping, Junking and Generating FAST Cash

Best Venison Recipes

Party Time Chicken Wings Recipes and Bonus Dip Recipes

Summer time Sangria

And many more!

A Little Info about This Book and About Me

Hello! Diana Loera here with a new book for fellow authors.

You may have read one, two or all three of my What I Did to Sell More Kindle Books on Amazon books.

I create most of the softcover versions of my books, including this one, in an 8 ½ by 11 format as I don't like squinting at tiny font in a tiny book.

I began writing and publishing books a couple years ago after wanting to become a full time author for several years.

I've been in the direct response (infomercial) industry for about 20 years. I loved the work that I did but the industry has been changing over the years and I predict even more changes in the next five years.

As I looked ahead, I really wanted to write and publish my own books and do so full time. When I shared this idea with several trusted colleagues, I was nicely told to keep doing what I was doing and why on earth would I want to leave a business that I knew backwards and forwards. On top of that, I had built from scratch a profitable company so in my colleagues' opinions, I should forget my crazy pipe dream and stick to what I knew.

But, as you see – I didn't.

The one really big plus point that I had going for me is that I know how to market. I have been able to apply my marketing knowledge to my book marketing and it continues to pay off.

I still handle some advertising, mainly for long time clients or referrals from long time clients, but the core part of my business is writing my books, marketing them and helping fellow authors market their books.

I wrote three marketing books for authors and have two more author books in the works now (plus four more other books in the works).

This book was actually the most recently started book for authors. I bumped it ahead of my other two books due to receiving several emails from other authors asking me about Pinterest marketing and then noticing my own success of Pinterest pinning = book sales in the same day.

In this book, we look at the third most popular social media vehicle – Pinterest.

Pinterest drives a lot of my book sales and I have my assistant pinning every week. I built my boards from scratch and just recently added Pinterest marketing to my assistant's weekly work flow.

I truly think Pinterest is the hidden pile of gold nuggets in the mining shaft of marketing options. The biggest challenge that you have – is you need to get in the mine shaft and grab your share of those nuggets before the Author Gold Rush descends upon that mining shaft

I started using Pinterest much more than I had before and during that month I noticed that my book sales doubled.

I attribute the doubling to Pinterest marketing being combined with my regular marketing.

In this book we are going to walk through Pinterest with our end goal being when we wrap up you are using Pinterest to your advantage.

This book was originally planned as the beginning steps for developing a presence on Pinterest.

As I created this book, I noticed the impact of video marketing and how it also increased sales.

I decided to merge the two together – Pinterest and Video Marketing- as interestingly enough- they can easily work hand in hand to increase book sales. In this book you will find out exactly what I am referring to and how to use both Pinterest and Video Marketing to your advantage.

I debated regarding writing a second book just on Video Marketing after I finished one on just Pinterest Marketing but decided to offer the two together. In other words – you are getting two books in one.

My success with Pinterest and Video Marketing should not be used to gauge your own personal success. You may have better results than I have or that may not be the case.

Marketing is a commitment and if you want to achieve book sales, you need to market or have someone working on marketing for you.

This is a book for beginning with Pinterest and Video Marketing – the goal of this book is to get your feet wet and start with the beginning marketing steps.

My books are all non- fiction at this time but I do think that fiction authors will also be able to use the information in this book to start to establish themselves on Pinterest and utilize video effectively.

If you are already actively pinning away on Pinterest and are seeing consistent book sales and/or seeing solid sales from video marketing, this book may not be for you unless you are like me and read anything you can find as often you find a tip or tool that you somehow missed before.

Table of Contents

Introduction

You've probably heard the buzz about Pinterest marketing. You may already have a Pinterest account and have found it is a cool way to discover great recipes and DIY ideas and dragonfly pics and butterfly pics and hairstyle pics and the list continues on and on as there are millions of pins to choose from.

But when it comes to marketing your book and Pinterest – you may still be wondering how Pinterest can benefit you and how to harness the power of Pinterest to make book sales for you.

My name is Diana Loera. I've been a marketer for over 20 years. I've bought millions of dollars in advertising for some of the most popular infomercials in history.

When I began buying infomercial advertising, the Internet was a somewhat vague idea for marketing and then grew into what it is now – the Wild, Wild West of marketing complete with some shady characters in the midst of the Gold Rush.

Pinterest caught my attention a couple years ago and I began building my Pinterest board. I was a casual Pinterest user. In other words, I'd pin for hours one day and not even look at Pinterest for weeks.

Yet in the back of my mind, as a marketer, I knew there was potential to use Pinterest as a vehicle to make sales.

I decided to follow my dream of becoming an author and started moving into writing almost full time. That was in 2011. I still handle TV and radio marketing for certain long time clients and Pinterest stayed on my radar since 2011, even if on the back burner.

When I began publishing books, I hired someone to do a little Pinterest work for me and I did see enough sales activity to make me curious. When my pinner retired I had a hard time finding someone to replace him.

I still see sales from those original pins – this is the staying power of Pinterest at work and one more reason that it is important to authors.

Fast forward to earlier this week. I now have a full time virtual assistant who works with me 5 to 7 days a week. One of her key projects is pinning on Pinterest for me.

On Monday morning, as I do every morning, I checked my book sales. I noticed two brand new books both had 3 sales each. I had asked my assistant to pin images for the two books and she had done so while I was asleep. She is located in a country with a time zone the opposite of mine which works well as when I sleep she works so it is basically as though I have doubled my productivity.

But, let me get back to the topic of Pinterest. We'll discuss virtual assistants in another book.

So in less than a couple hours, I had generated 6 book sales – solely due to Pinterest.

I am hoping this fact has made you sit upright and want to know more. If not, no worries – just keep reading and by the time we wrap up this book, I think you'll be as gung ho about Pinterest as I am.

Some author contact me and ask for help with Pinterest. Other authors say to me that they know they should be on Pinterest but……..how does it work and how am I making consistent sales? The last group of authors haven't even thought about Pinterest and are not active on it at all.

It doesn't matter which, if any, of the above groups that you fall in.

Pinterest may be one of the best opportunities for authors to expand their potential audience reach, increase awareness and make book sales.

Pinterest is growing non -stop and is now on the radar of the majority of marketing agencies as a solid marketing tool.

The plus point is – Pinterest is a free tool. Yes you need to build your presence but there is no sign up cost and no monthly fee.

It is easy to set up and use – the key though is understanding several key steps to help you gain traction fast.

Otherwise, it is amazingly easy to get swept away by the sheer volume of pins and spends hours, having fun, but accomplishing little.

On the flip side, while almost anyone can create a Pinterest pin, there are proven things that you should be doing to maximize your leverage.

If you aren't quite sure what Pinterest is – imagine a bulletin board. Then imagine yourself pinning cards on the board.

Cards with recipes, quotes, beautiful images, butterflies, dragonflies, hot rod cars, fashion- the list is practically endless.

Now if you were doing this on a real bulletin board, you would soon be out of room and organizing would not be fun. But thanks to the beauty of the Internet, you and millions of others can create a virtual bulletin board and pin to your heart's delight.

70 MILLION – yes, you read the number correctly 70 million people are on Pinterest as of January 2015.

So with 70 million people on Pinterest – the odds are good that it is an ideal place to market your books and make book sales.

But let's take this one step farther as far as marketing –

I'm sure you noticed the mention of Video Marketing and we will be discussing it in this book.

I have set this book up so that we discuss Pinterest, discuss Video Marketing and then we loop back to Pinterest and marketing.

Pinterest and Video Marketing make an amazing pair and I am really eager to get other authors up to speed on the potential of both Pinterest and Video Marketing and even more so, about combining the two.

As far as Video Marketing, in my case, I found that adding properly created video to my marketing resulted in sales increasing, even sales from outside the United States.

Video Marketing is not complicated and like Pinterest, has been fairly untapped so it offers a prime marketing turf for authors.

I should add – if you've read any of my other books you know that I prefer to write as though we are discussing marketing over a cup of coffee or tea. I like to keep a relaxed pace and make marketing a fun experience.

Later in this book, you'll come across my email address. You are more than welcome to email me if you have marketing questions once you've finished this book.

I'm also going to share a few of my sources. You are welcome to find your own sources but I find that the best way to be successful is to duplicate the successful actions of others versus re-inventing the wheel.

Pinterest Users are Buyers

Marketers have noticed that Pinterest is generating more traffic to sites than the ever popular Twitter.

That is not to say don't use Twitter. You should have a solid mix of marketing tools including Twitter and Pinterest.

One difference between sharing things on Twitter and Pinterest is that most times people are able to see exactly what the item is before they click on it.

Plus eye-catching photos and images have a way of attracting attention much better than singling out one tweet in a mass flood of tweets.

But the fact does stand that Pinterest is driving traffic to web sites and currently it is out producing Twitter.

Over 20 percent of Pinterest users have purchased an item that they found via Pinterest. I find this to be an impressive percentage.

Before you scoff at the idea of 20 percent being impressive, please let me share a couple pieces of information.

As someone who has managed large ad campaigns, it is natural for a client to think everyone who sees his widget is going to buy it. That is definitely not the case. Millions of people may be sitting in from of a TV when Spin Mop flashes their two minute commercial.

On average, it takes around 20 airings before a person actually notices the commercial. You read that right. It takes about 20 times before a person actually notices a commercial.

Think about it. Can you list the last ten commercials that you saw on TV selling something?

It takes repetition before a TV ad campaign starts to attract attention which is why many ad campaigns flop.

Then we have the addition of Tivo and let's remember the old fashioned concept of using commercial time to clear the dishes, get a soda, use the washroom or in a more modern time, check your texts and emails.

With Pinterest, we have people on Pinterest actively looking. The Pinterest browsers are a captive audience. They are scrolling through pins looking for cool stuff to pin.

Remember- 70 million people are on Pinterest.

Pinterest User Demographics

Currently, the majority of those on Pinterest are females but the number of males is growing fast. In the US – a little over 80 percent of users are females.

The most popular interest of Pinterest users surveyed is Cooking/Recipes.

This is followed by:

Home decorating

Crafts

Quotes

Fashion

Entertainment

Gardening

If you are a fiction writer, you may be thinking that how on earth can you tie this in to your books? I understand your question and we will be covering how authors of fiction and non-fiction can harness the power of Pinterest.

How Often Do People Utilize Pinterest?

37% of people surveyed log in a few times a week, with only 10% saying that they use the site a few times a day.

These people are all active on the site, having created at least 1 – 10 boards themselves.

This shows us that people are not just coming to look around, they are getting involved. They are pinning to their own boards and others are seeing pins and repining.

While Pinterest users are considerably less than Facebook users and Twitter users they are actively on Pinterest and provide a demographic that is proven to buy books and other products after seeing them on Pinterest.

Pinterest is currently the fastest growing social media platform and that means that for once – you are able to get in on the ground floor and ride the Pinterest wave as it grows.

What interests me as an author and as a marketer is that it is possible to generate considerable sales via Pinterest marketing. The pins that you place circulate and continue to circulate months and even years later.

This then brings up to the question you are probably already thinking – so how do we encourage them to buy our books?

Let's continue on to the next chapter and start discussing our marketing strategy. Please remember, we are in the beginning phase of starting your Pinterest marketing – right now we are building your Pinterest foundation.

Interesting fact – over 80 percent of all pins being circulated on any given day are re-pins.

Think on this for a minute please.

80 percent of all pins are re-pins.

While we want people to see and re-pin our pins – let's also keep in mind that adding a new pin means your pin is one of only 20 percent of the new ones and is fresh content.

Unlike Twitter, where we do not want to do me, me, me tweets non -stop, with Pinterest we can promote our books.

We do want to add variety to our promotions.

In the case of non- fiction books we may have a bit more options for images that we can use.

Fiction writers do have some good options too, it just may require thinking a bit about your book, your readers and what images could mesh well with your book.   We'll discuss this a bit more soon.

What is important with Pinterest marketing is to create a reason that makes people want to not only re-pin your pin but click through to your site.

Our goal is to intrigue a person enough that they spot our pin in the sea of pins.

The first step is using quality images.

Based on research, lighter images are repined 20 times more than darker images.

Images without faces get re-pinned over 20 percent more than those with faces.

While you can pin your book cover, I also highly suggest using other images too.

You want to build a curiosity and interest so the viewer clicks through. If you reveal what is behind the screen – there is no curiosity to click through to your site.

Creating Your Pinterest Profile

There are two types of Pinterest accounts – Personal and Business.

For now, I suggest that you create your account as a Personal account.

Later, you can determine if you want to switch to a Business account. Switching from Personal to Business is fairly easy.

I don't think that at this time you can switch the other way – from Business to Personal. I searched online and found nothing on the topic so let's play it safe and start with a Personal account.

Once you are seeing a significant stream of income that you can attribute to Pinterest, then you may want to review Pinterest's overview of Personal versus Business accounts and move into Business when the time is right.

The Business account will also give you access to Pinterest Analytics but our focus at this time to develop an established presence on Pinterest.

Your Pinterest Profile is a valuable piece of marketing real estate.

Your user name should, ideally, include your author name or company.

As an author you want to create a professional yet personable profile. I suggest including a photo of yourself. You'll see that my photo is currently one that shows my husband as well as myself.

I talk about my husband in some of my books and he has been a key part of several of my making money in a down economy books.

If I wrote stories about pets, then perhaps I would include photo of myself with my cat. But in my situation, it was a natural choice to include my husband in the photo that I use as my profile pic.

My goal is to give readers a look inside my world. I'm interested in finding out more about people who read my books. Many readers email me with questions and I enjoy chatting with them via email. I want to build rapport with people who read my books because they are the reason that I select certain topics and write about them.

I definitely suggest adding a photo- don't leave it blank.

On your Pinterest profile, there is a space to list your website.

As an author, you do need to have some type of website. If you do not have one yet then set up your Pinterest account starting today and plan on getting to work on your website immediately.

I know I am asking you to please do two things immediately- create a Pinterest account and a website, but if you want to market – you need a website and you need to utilize Pinterest.

You may be wondering -what is the point of doing all of this work?

This is going to help you create more user engagement and traffic.

In this book, we are setting the stage and getting the beginning steps done.

Once you are set up and start pinning, this will become a much easier task.

When your website is verified, you will see it on your Pinterest page along with a red check mark symbolizing that your website is verified.

Pinners can find out about you faster as they will have your website link right in front of them.

But the largest perk is this step will help boost your online visibility and also help with SEO (search engine optimization).

When you click on your profile, you'll see that there is a box marked verify website.

When you click on the box you will be directed to two options for doing the site verification.

My website is a Go Daddy website and it was a bit of a challenge to get my Pinterest account verified but I did some online research and finally found the correct information regarding Pinterest verification for Go Daddy websites.

I am not a computer wizard but I was determined to get the verification process done as my research showed that verification is important.

With Pinterest - You also need to check your settings. This is an easy step – just go to top right of your screen, click on your photo/name and then click Settings. You want to ensure that your 'Search Privacy' setting is marked as No.

This step, even though it is very simple, is vey important. It allows search engines to display your Pinterest profile in search results. Google indexes Pinterest content and, interestingly enough, it is easier to get your Pinterest profile ranked in Google than your blog.

Before Google started doing frequent algorithm changes, I could flip a blog together and rank quite high in search. Now we need to think outside the box a bit to get the desired search rankings needed and this is one way to do so.

If you do not have a website at this time, remember to come back and do the steps above as soon as your website is up and running.

Creating Your Boards on Pinterest

In the beginning, you may feel a bit stressed as you look at an empty Pinterest page.

The main thing is – get started.

What do you like? Let's say antiques and stained glass come to mind.

Create two boards – Antiques and Stained Glass.

Later, you can go back and change the names of your boards as you see fit. Antiques is a rather broad search term and ideally, you'll break the Antiques board into more something more refined such as Antique Glassware, Carnival Glass, Antique Spittoons or whatever the case may be but at this time, versus mulling this over for a week, I'd like you to get started today so if something is general – so be it. Later you can modify.

Find some cool pins to pin to your boards.

Follow some or all of the Pinterest accounts where you found your pins. The odds are good that they will follow you back.

Now let's start zoning in on who we want to attract.

Let's say that you write romance books.

What ties in with Romance?

Create boards to reflect the tie- ins.

Ideally, you want to start thinking about keywords.

Let's start thinking about your target audience.

If you are a romance writer, you want to attract romance readers.

What do your readers like?

What are they pinning on their own boards?

Determining your target audience is not going to happen in an hour.

This is your end goal.

For now, let's plan on starting with 5 to 10 boards.

Our first goal is to get 20 quality pins and re-pins on each of those boards.

Our second goal is to get 50 quality pins and re-pins on those boards

You are simply going to re-pin pins that you like on to your boards.

You'll be adding some of your own pins too.

You can use the search box at the top of the Pinterest site to help you with this step.

I like the search box as you can look for pinners as well as pins. It is easy to get swept away as you look at all the cool pins but try to stay on task and get your boards set up as fast as possible.

We also want to create an Author Board to showcase your books. Ideally, pins will include your book cover images, your book trailers, your book video reviews and an infographic or two (we will discuss infographics in detail later in this book)

You also want to add a description for each board and select the best category.

You can change your description and category if needed later but the main thing we want to do is start the ball rolling.

You'll find your Pinterest boards grow and your ideas develop as you progress.

As your boards grow and as others start to re-pin you'll be able to see what interests people and what they like to re-pin. This will give you some insight regarding what they may like to see on your board.

I'll try to remember to mention this again in this book but while I'm thinking of it – once you have your board started, you are welcome to email me at LoeraPublishing@hotmail.com

Put Pinterest Help in the subject line or something along that topic – Pinterest Question is another choice.

I receive a lot of emails weekly, if you do not hear back in a week, do not feel bad about emailing me a second time. Usually I am pretty good with responding quickly but sometimes I miss an email or it lands in the spam folder.

If you email me be sure to include a link to your Pinterest board, tell me about your books and then you and I will brainstorm a bit about Pinterest.

You are also welcome to email me with a link to your Pinterest boards, even if you do not have any marketing questions, and I will follow your boards.

Pin Creation Ideas for Authors

You may be thinking that sure, if you are a non- fiction writer, there are plenty of pin options but how about fiction authors?

Regardless of if you write fiction or non -fiction – quotes are hot.

Let's take this one step further –

Quotes from your characters.

Quote pins are very popular and are a hot re-pin.

Let's say that your romance genre is set in the Deep South.

Using a haunting image of foggy mists and trees in the swamp – if this is the location of your story- along with an enticing quote is one that may attract attention.

I also suggest using the free tool Quozio to turn quotations into visual pins with text.

www.Quozio.com

If your book features non- fiction work such as recipes, use one of your recipe photos as a pin.

Below the image, you will add text.

Lesson learned from experience – I would not suggest using FREE during such and such dates. For starters, when your pin resurfaces in three years, it will appear outdated.

Secondly, your end goal is for someone to buy your book not to have what I call moochers – those who will grab up ANYTHING because it is free but never look at it again or write a review. You want to build a loyal reader base and you want book sales.

For your pin copy you want something catchy – such as Haunting mists, romance and a tangled web of lies await you.

See how I am painting the picture and drawing the viewer in to click out of curiosity.

A book quote is also a solid choice.

I do not add things like – 3.99 on Amazon. I want to build intrigue and persuade the viewer to click the image.

When one clicks the image, they are then taken to whatever website that you imbed.

Do not imbed an affiliate link. Pinterest currently strips affiliate links out of the pins.

How to Create a Pin

This is a basic overview of the steps that you need to do to create your own pins.

You can create a pin by uploading an image from your computer or website.

Make sure you are not infringing upon copyright with images. We will discuss sources for images later in this book.

STEP 1

Log in to your Pinterest account

On the home page, in the top right, you will click on the PLUS SIGN button. You will see it on the lower right- it is circled with red on the image below.

You will then be offered 3 choices –Upload a Pin, Pin from a Website and Create a Board.

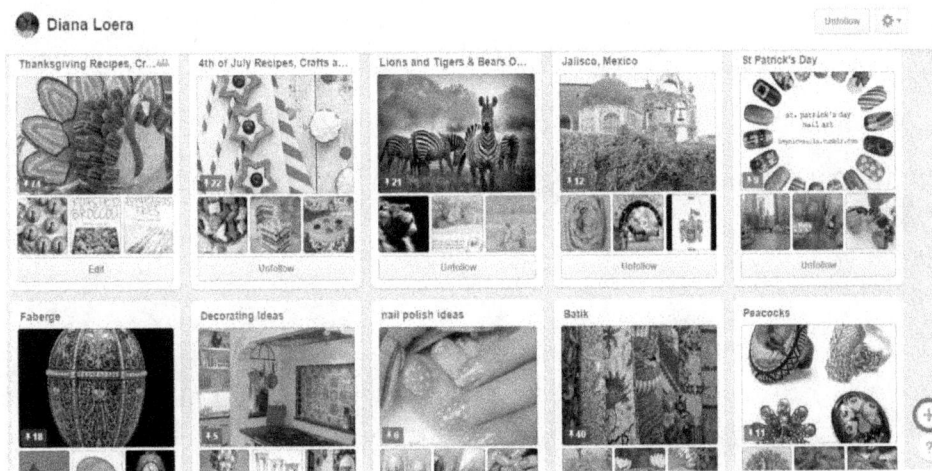

If you are pinning an image from a website, then you will choose the Upload a Pin option

Get the Pinterest browser button to save creative ideas from around the web.

⬆ (Upload a Pin)

🌐 Pin from a website

▦ Create a board

You will then be shown a new box where you can choose image from your file.

Upload an Image   ✕

Choose Image

If you are pinning an image from a website, then you will choose the Pin from a website option

Get the Pinterest browser button to save creative ideas from around the web.

⬆ Upload a Pin

🌐 (Pin from a website)

▦ Create a board

You will then be shown a new box where you can type in the url of a website. After providing the web url, click find images.

Pin from a website

×

Tip: To save links quicker, get the Pinterest browser button.

| http://... | Next |

On the new page, Choose an image to create a Pin. The second one from the left on the top row below is highlighted to show you what you will see.

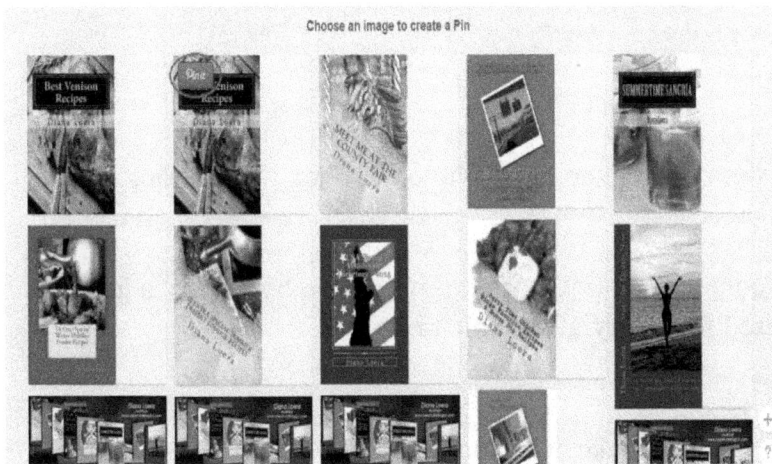

Once you've found the image, click the pin it button on the upper left side of the image.

Then below the board's name, provide a description of the image. You may also wish to include a Hashtag here (in your description).

Pick a board

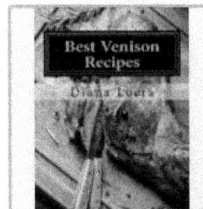

| Board | Best Venison Recipes |
| Description | What's this Pin all about? |

Post to Twitter   Close   Pin it

Click Pin It when you're done.

Finding Images to Pin

Remember that when pinning, there are guidelines that you do need to follow.

You cannot use copyrighted info that belongs to someone else.

You do not want to create spammy links

If you are re-pinning something, give credit to the original pinner – as in do not remove our change their comments.

Always provide a good pin description.

Pin quality images.

If you are pinning images other than your book cover, book photos or book illustrations, then you can purchase royalty free images

I use two sources www.DreamsTime.com and www.DepositPhotos.com   both carry a great selection of images that can be purchased for a very affordable price.

I am not an affiliate of either company not do I make any money by referring readers to these companies. I like both companies as I have found a great variety of images on them that are royalty free and are quality images.

You can also use quotes that you create.

You will be adding video to your Pinterest boards too but you also want a good amount of quality images. We will be covering videos next.

New Marketing Ground on Pinterest

You can also post videos on Pinterest – such as book trailers and video book reviews.

Video Book Reviews are the hottest thing since sliced bread.

Video Book Reviews on Pinterest is still very new and therefor stand out.

People who view videos are 85 percent MORE inclined to buy than those who do not view a video.

That statistic alone is enough reason to do a video book review.

But let's dig even deeper -

In 2013, ReelSEO released their Video Marketing Survey and Business Trends Report, which incorporated feedback from over 600 marketing respondents. They discovered the following:

93% of marketers are using video in their campaigns

84% are using video for website marketing

60% are using video for email marketing

70% are optimizing video for search engines

70% will increase their spend on video

82% confirmed that video had a positive impact on their business

Obviously, video marketing works.

But let's dig even deeper into these statistics –

There are companies such as ReelSEO and Wistia and big players like YouTube who are analyzing these numbers around the clock – why?

Because they know they have an untapped source that is relatively new to the public and it is making money, money, money.

Before we talk about video marketing, we need to take a look at video engagement.

One frequently mentioned statistic is that viewer engagement has to happen within the first 10 seconds of watching a video.

This gold nugget of wisdom has been corroborated by the National Center for Biotechnology Information, which reports that the average attention span in 2013 was 9 seconds, one second less than the attention span of a goldfish.

You read that correctly – 9 seconds.

This is another reason that repetition is so important in marketing.

On the other hand, the longer a video runs, the lower its retention of viewers.

Videos under 1 minute enjoy 80% viewer retention up to the 30-second mark, while videos 2-3 minutes in length still enjoy 60% retention.

Videos that are 5-10 minutes in length, which really is about the maximum you should consider for online video marketing purposes, see over 50% viewer retention halfway through.

Please understand 100 percent viewer retention is not our goal. We are not out to re-invent the wheel – we are out to produce viewer engagement which the end result is a sale.

How Important is Video Marketing?

Diode Digital found that **video promotion is 600% more effective than print and direct mail combined.** I typed this and bolded it as it is such an incredible piece of data.

They also found that, before reading any text, 60% of site visitors will watch a video if available.

When I find data like the above I want to scream it from the rooftop as this is gold for authors. But, let's continue with a few more facts -

Viewers remember videos better too.

Online Publishers Association noticed – and this fact goes back to 2007- that 80% of viewers recall a video ad they have seen in the past 30 days.

26% of viewers then look for more info about the product, 22% visit the product site, 15% visit the brand site, and 12% make the purchase.

None of this is really surprising when you take into account that one minute of video is worth 1.8 million words according to Forrester Research.

Maximizing Video Marketing

Your video book review can be used in numerous places besides Pinterest and this is one reason that I like the added power of creating a video book review and book trailers.

I can place the videos on Pinterest and maximize the video by using it in other marketing.

The first and most obvious place to incorporate video is your website.

The home page, landing pages, blog posts, etc., any page is fair game for video enhancement, and the data proves it.

Landing pages with video lead to 800% more conversion (this data is from FunnelScience).

In fact, 88% of visitors stay longer on a site with prominent video displayed (this data is according to MistMedia).

Those that stay longer spend an average of 120 seconds more on a retail site and are 64% more likely to purchase after viewing a single product video (this data is according to comScore).

52% of shoppers confess that watching product videos makes them more confident in making a purchase (this data is according to Invodo).

40% of shoppers will even visit a store online or in-person after watching a video (this data is according to Google).

Online Publishers Association backs this up with a similar finding that 46% of surveyed shoppers would be more likely to seek out additional information about a product after seeing an online video.

Social Media marketing is enhanced by adding your video book review and book trailer.

According to Simply Measured, video is shared 1200% more times than links and text combined.

Diode Digital also discovered that 60% of viewers will watch video before reading any site text, and will share their experience when presented with a "share this video" button.

Even more encouraging, Invodo reports that 92% of mobile video viewers share video.

By now, you are probably thinking about how fast you can get your video book reviews and book trailers online.

This is where it gets really good – despite all of the facts on conversion rates and viewer retention, many people have been very slow to get on the video marketing rocketship.

We know video is useful for social media engagement, yet the number of videos being shared on social media is significantly lower than you'd expect.

Back in 2011, while 71% of companies were on Facebook and 59% were on Twitter, only 33% were on YouTube (UMass Dartmouth).

Pinterest was still in the beginning stages as far as companies having an interest in using it as a marketing vehicle.

The numbers tell the story: video marketing hasn't been as readily adopted as other forms of content marketing – yet.

Once you have pinned your videos on Pinterest, you can then leverage all the possibilities that you have to further boost your book marketing.

This of course brings us to the mother lode of all videos – YouTube.

ReelSEO's YouTube statistics for 2012 gives us an interesting piece of information to ponder - 500 years' worth of YouTube video are watched on Facebook every day.

It's no surprise that YouTube is the world's second biggest search engine after Google, or that YouTube accounts for 28% of all Google searches.

500 years' worth of video a day translates into 3042 hours' worth of video watched simultaneously across the world each second.

Do you see where I am going with this info?

You can use the video that you are placing on Pinterest to reach even more possible book buyers with just a few simple marketing additions.

According to YouTube, more than 1 billion viewers watch its videos each month, clocking over 6 billion hours.

One hour of video is uploaded to YouTube each second.

100 hours are uploaded each minute.

More videos are uploaded to YouTube in one month than the 3 major US networks have created in the past 60 years.

Robert Kyncl, Google's Vice President and Global Head of Business at You Tube, stated that video will soon be 90% of all Internet traffic.

I think we can agree that he makes a valid point.

Interestingly enough, over 80% of YouTube traffic actually comes from outside the US, pointing to a huge global viewership many businesses haven't even begun to tap.

I know firsthand about traffic from outside the US as many of my book sales come from countries besides the United States. They come from sales made due to – you know it – videos.

Not surprising is the fact that mobile views make up more than 25 percent of YouTube's global watch time, which brings us to yet another video marketing channel – mobile.

Many laptop and desktop viewers only stick with video for 2 minutes or less, while mobile users are more patient.

iPhone users watch 2.4 minutes on average, Androids users give 3 minutes of their time, Symbian users 4 minutes, and iPad users 5 minutes (according to Visible Measures).

Translated into percentages, mobile and tablet shoppers are 300% as likely to view a video as laptop/desktop users (this data is from Invodo).

I have watched this area grow extremely fast over the last few years. I have talked with all clients planning on airing infomercials to let them know their website (with a commercial imbedded) needs to be mobile viewer friendly as mobile viewers are growing extremely fast.

Online video is about 50% of all mobile traffic (according to Bytemobile Mobile Analytics Report), and is predicted to become 75% of all mobile data traffic by 2016 (this data is according to Cisco).

It is certainly understandable that mobile viewers would be very accustomed to using their mobile devices to watch video.

It would also support the fact that 92% of mobile viewers share videos.

Watching videos via a mobile is an untapped area and here we are with our books. It doesn't get any better than this does it? We are at the front of the Gold Rush.

Marketing a Video via Email

If you have an established email list that you market to – this fact is one you should know –

Videos in email have been shown to increase click-through rates by over 96% on the first introductory email (according to an Implix Email Marketing Trends Survey).

GetResponse reported similar numbers with its observation that emails with video have a 5.6% higher open rate and a 96.4% higher click-through rate.

The effect video has on press releases is even more impressive: multimedia press releases with video are viewed 970% more than text-only (according to PR Newswire).

Put another way, email subscriber dropout is reduced by 75% with the incorporation of video (according to Eloqua).

Power Tip - emails with the word "video" in the subject line are opened 7% more often (according to Experian).

Needless to say, never ever spam people. If you do not have an established relationship with a person, you should not be mailing advertising to them. I'm sure that you know this but just wanted to mention it as a reminder.

To sum it up, video is everywhere these days, and with a very good reason as we've just read.

Now is the best time to start taking video marketing seriously.

Let's first look at Video Book Reviews.

A video book review is a professionally produced video about your book.

There is a HUGE difference in writing a book review and writing a script for a video book review.

Your script needs to flow naturally and contain certain keywords.

The individual doing the book review needs to have a clear and concise speaking voice.

I highly suggest the talent has English as a first language unless your book is culturally slanted towards readers from another country.

You also need the correct talent.

If your book is a fast paced steamy erotic read, I wouldn't suggest using a male senior citizen as the talent.

If your book is a travel guide, well, depending on your target audience, the senior citizen male may be an option.

You want to engage your current followers and attract new followers all who are re-pinning your pins so that their followers see them and re-pin.

You also want a quality video that can get some lift outside of Pinterest.

So with all of this being said – let's look at three video book reviews. All three are using the same talent.

http://youtu.be/reBvilfCh5Y

http://youtu.be/RSpF9td-Rg4

http://youtu.be/ZJ1QKn1oGMk

The talent is articulate and she is expressive.

I don't know if she uses a teleprompter or not but her speech flows smoothly.

She does not sound stiff or look nervous.

She presents with the versatility needed to reach Pinterest viewers, You Tube viewers and email viewers. This is hugely important as we want to maximize the use of each video as much as possible. We also want to build repetition which builds branding.

All three of the videos were created by

http://www.verifiedebookreviews.com/video-book-reviews.html

Needless to say, you can also look for your own source but please remember, you are better off duplicating a successful action versus trying to reinvent the wheel.

The three examples listed are exactly that- examples. You may end up with different talent but the main thing is, you are allowing experts to handle this project versus taking up hours and hours of your own time that could be spent writing.

As someone who utilizes an assistant daily I also have learned firsthand – Penny wise, pound foolish.

This doesn't mean that those who have less money are smarter or that being penny wise is good. Instead it refers to a person who goes to great lengths to save some money (penny wise) but ends up losing money (pound foolish) in the long run.

For example – you know now how valuable video can be with marketing.

You know that you want to do a video book review.

You decide you will just do it yourself.

You ask dear Aunt Bertha to be your talent.

Aunt Bertha, while a delightful lady, is not camera savvy – at all.

So after ten retakes, three that have her cat sashaying across the desk, and one with Uncle Elmer walking in to the camera……you have at best, an amateur video.

I learned some time ago that really you sometimes have to just admit to yourself there are some things you are better off paying for than trying to do yourself.

Along with that realization came my acceptance of needing a full time assistant.

Now I am lot more relaxed and instead of trying to do it all myself, I focus mainly on writing and leave the projects to others.

Unless you are a professional in the video industry, this is one example of letting someone else handle the project.

I searched for video book reviewers and the woman in the video book reviews that you just watched stood out considerably above others.

Time is money. While you are sifting through video talent options, your competition is contacting a reviewer, perhaps even the reviewer we just watched, having a video created and will be pinning their video before you've found talent to do your video review.

I'm sure there are definitely other options available but the main thing is – take action and get a video done immediately.

Video Book Trailers

A video trailer of your book is another must do marketing step.

I've found 30 seconds to be an ideal length but I also suggest testing 60 second trailers and possibly 120 second trailers to see what length resonates best with your target audience.

A trailer can drive traffic. Like a video book review, you can use a video book trailer in numerous marketing pieces including YouTube, your website and Pinterest.

Video book trailers can have a VO (voice over) and/or music.

I like to use a mix of stock images, book cover image and key phrases.

If you would like input on a book trailer or to find out the people that I recommend for book trailer creation, please contact me via email. Thank you.

Driving Traffic with the Pinterest Widget

Pinterest has a cool widget that you can create by using their widget builder.

You can increase your Pinterest traffic by notifying people who visit your website about your Pinterest account.

The image below is a screenshot of one of my sites. This one is for www.Swingbellys.com and showcases some of my recipe books.

See the Pinterest widget on the right?

Adding a Pinterest widget helps you to build your Pinterest followers.

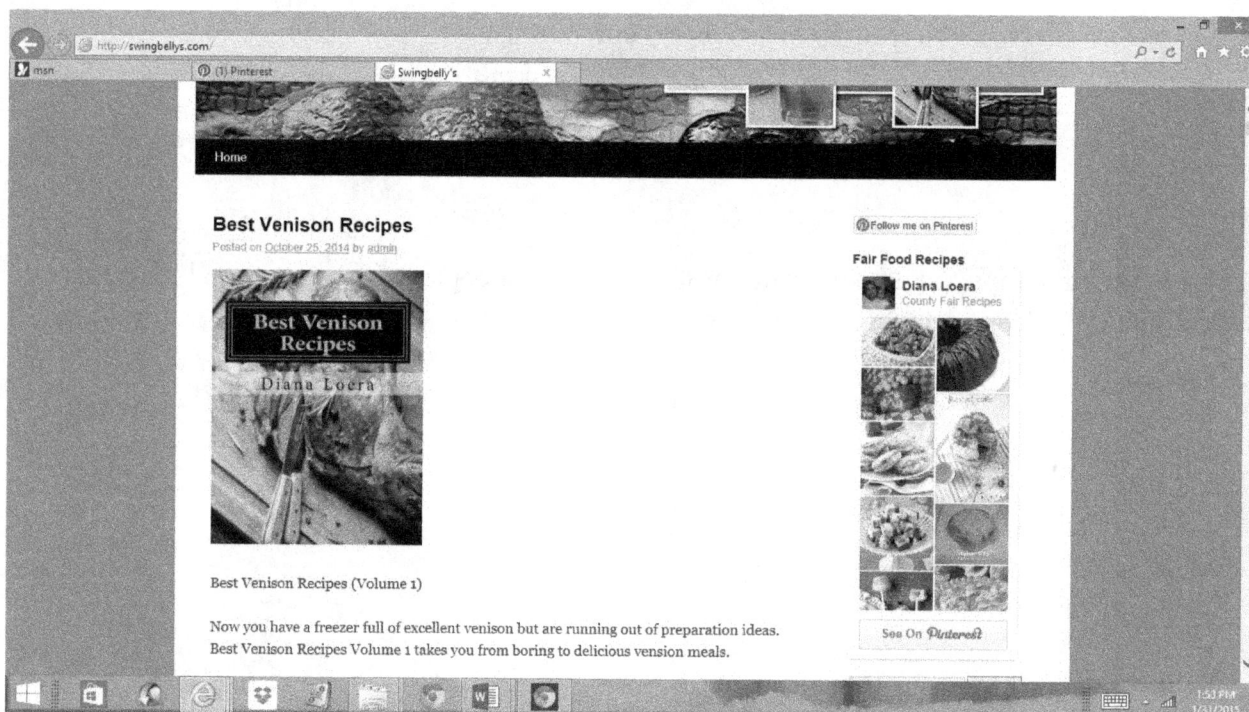

In case you are wondering – I have not added my book trailers to this site yet as I like the clean look of the site. I added the Pinterest widget (actually my awesome assistant added it) and have been pleased with the results.

I have a couple sites in the works for single books and on those sites I will add trailers and/or video book reviews. With multiple books on one page and a Pinterest widget, this site gives viewers options but not an overwhelm.

Creating a Pinning Schedule for Profit

As mentioned earlier, I determined that once I started having my assistant pin frequently, my book sales increased.

Her main focus is creating pins and pinning them. Her secondary focus is re-pinning.

Sometimes, when creating new pins, we use the same images with different copy.

Pins point to Amazon and then the same image and content points to my web site.

Please remember – I have more than one book – I have more than five books. Making serious money as an author is much easier when you have multiple books. It also gives me more options when pinning as you cannot keep pinning one book. You need to have as many books as possible on Pinterest.

Note – we were pinning and using www.LoeraPublishing.com. This site redirects to my site www.LoeraPublishingLLC.com so this week and moving forward, we will be point pins to Amazon and to the LLC domain. I am doing this for tracking purposes. If you use multiple domains and they point to one main domain, I suggest using the main domain.

She then also re-pins to help build my boards but the money comes from making and circulating pins from my books.

I also log on to re-pin occasionally but usually not more than once or twice a week as I have my assistant handling the project. I log on mainly because I enjoy Pinterest or if I have an idea and want to see what pins are on Pinterest regarding the topic already.

Since we do not want to just pin our own images we do need to also re-pin to build traffic and followers.

You do want to be selective about re-pins.

When my assistant first starting re-pinning for me I think she was very conservative regarding her re-pinning choices. I would rather have someone be conservative than pin pell-mell and have a sloppy messy board.

If you utilize an assistant for pinning, what I did in the beginning, was to spot check what she re-pinned. I then searched and found additional pins to re-pin.

She then was able to see what else she could re-pin. As we progressed, my additional re-pins decreased as she gained confidence.

You want to be known as the person with the class act Pinterest board. Being known for providing quality pins and re-pins will make you stand out.

I'd like to see you have a Pinterest presence5 to 7 days a week. Ito doesn't need to be hours – even 15 to 30 minutes will make a difference.

You will want to keep your boards organized. For example, if you have a board that is for Antiques and you have a lot of antique stained glass on it then I would suggest starting a second board for Antique Stained Glass.

DIY boards often end up evolving into multiple boards with smaller categories of DIY.

Flowers may end up being divided into multiple boards.

You want to ensure your board title is one that may be a good search term. I would create Breakfast Recipes versus Recipes.

Fourth of July Recipes over Recipes or Holiday Recipes.

I suggest doing a search for the title you are going to use. There is a search bar at the top of Pinterest. This may give you some ideas to refine your board title and also may help you find pins to pin to your new board.

As your boards grow in size, you may decide that you want to change the main cover image. Just hover your curser over the main image and select a new cover.

I suggest testing and measuring different descriptions. You may find that one description engages others to re-pin and also buy more so than other descriptions.

I also suggest creating two pins for each image and description. One pin will point to Amazon and one to your website.

If you ae using Google Analytics or a similar program (and you should be) you will be able to see what states/cities in the US and what countries are going to your website.

This is highly valuable data.

Ideally, you should be pinning consistently throughout the week. Five days a week spending fifteen minutes time each time is much better than 1 day a week for four hours straight.

Otherwise, you are bombarding people with a boatload of pins and then they don't hear from you for days. This is not an ideal way to build rapport and a good following.

Secret Boards on Pinterest

There has been a good amount of info and advice regarding Secret Boards.

Personally I do not use them at all.

Secret boards are boards that you create and no one else can see them. Or you can allow only select people to use them. If you are planning a wedding, surprise party or something along that line, I can see the value of a secret board. Otherwise, I have no other use for them.

Not too long ago, secret boards were touted as a way to keep your board under wraps until you had numerous pins on the board.

I have to disagree as more than once I have re-pinned an image that was the only image on that specific board.

If you want to gather images that you don't want others to see –then yes you can create a secret board but as far as our marketing goes – there isn't a reason to have one and definitely not because you only have an image or two on a board.

A Few Unique Pin Ideas

As you develop your boards remember that you want to add images that engage others and entice them to re-pin your images.

Engage your fans and future fans with a sneak peak of upcoming books.

Fiction authors– you can create boards for your book characters and/or the location where your book's story takes place. Recipes for the era of your story is another interesting idea.

Fiction and non-fiction authors-infographics can be eye catching and people will re-pin so they have the information at their fingertips.

Remember to keep your Pinterest board well rounded. You want to promote your books and also have other pins that interest others.

Mary Pinner may re-pin and follow your Beautiful Pink Roses board. She may re-pin your Rose Planting Tips infographic. Six months later, you may decide to switch from romance genre to mystery genre and Mary who loves mystery books but is so-so on romance reads may then click the buy button for your new mystery book.

You engaged Mary's interest with your common interest – Beautiful Pink Roses and built rapport with her. When she saw your mystery book image she was an eager buyer.

Moving Forward with Pinterest and Video Marketing

We've discussed creating videos and how you can maximize videos – Pinterest, web site, You Tube and even email.

While our main focus of this book has been Pinterest, I hope you see the great goldmine at the end of the tunnel that awaits you when you implement video marketing and Pinterest.

As I've mentioned in other books, you need to have more than one book in play. If you only have one book at this time, definitely start building your Pinterest and video marketing campaigns and please work to get multiple books published.

Having multiple books available gives your potential readers more options and also gives you more marketing options. But don't let that stop you from making multiple videos and multiple pins – just don't overload your board with pins for one or two books.

I'll be back with another book on more advanced Pinterest marketing in the near future. I also will soon have a book available regarding marketing to libraries.

My goal is to be able to help and boost fellow authors by sharing my marketing expertise.

Please remember, you are welcome to contact me LoeraPublishing@hotmail.com if you have questions about Pinterest or video marketing.

I'd also appreciate your feedback about this book and would love to hear about your success stories also.

Thank you for taking the time to read my book. I look forward to seeing YOUR book on Pinterest!

Sincerely,

Diana

www.ingramcontent.com/pod-product-compliance
Lightning Source LLC
Chambersburg PA
CBHW051235200326
41519CB00025B/7385